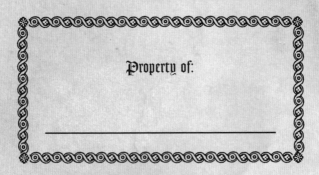

Property of:

_____

Oath of the Night's Watch

✿✿✿✿✿✿

Night gathers, and now my watch begins. It shall not end until my death. I shall take no wife, hold no lands, father no children. I shall wear no crowns and win no glory. I shall live and die at my post. I am the sword in the darkness. I am the watcher on the walls. I am the shield that guards the realm of men. I pledge my life and honor to the Night's Watch, for this night and all the nights to come.

HBO™

HOME BOX OFFICE.

INSIGHTS

INSIGHT ◉ EDITIONS

San Rafael, California

www.insighteditions.com